COLORADO BOY BREWERY:
Standard Operating Procedures

Also by Tom Hennessy

Frankenbrew—Build a Brewery For Under $20,000 (DVD)
Fabjob Guide to Become a Coffee House Owner
Fabjob Guide to Become a Restaurant Owner
Brewery Operations Manual: Three Steps to Open and Run a Successful Brewery

Colorado Boy Brewery: Standard Operating Procedures

Tom Hennessy

Tom Hennessy Publishing
2016

.

First Printing: 2016

ISBN 978-1-944784-14-0

Tom Hennessy Publishing
320 E. Main St.
Montrose, CO 81432

www.breweryoperationsmanual.com

Contents

Acknowledgements

This is a book I should have written a long time ago. In the Colorado Boy Immersion Course that we teach, we demonstrate how to do all the things needing to get done in the brewery, but nowhere are these things written down. One day, one of our students, Steve Stowell, of Triple S Brewing in Colorado Springs, casually said, "You should write all these procedures into an SOP manual." Well Steve, it took me long enough, but finally here it is. Thanks for the great idea!

I would also like to thank Colorado Boy Brewers Elliott Bell and Steve Wood, for letting me get in their way while taking pictures. To our brewery owners and Immersion Course teachers, Daniel and Dennis Richards of Echo Brewing and Colorado Boy Brewing, and to Nathaniel Miller of Big Choice Brewing, I also say thank you.

While I appreciate all of the feedback I have received from brewers across the country, I would especially like to thank my peers who took the time to review this manual: Randy King, Matt Cowart, Ro Guenzel, Jason Weissburg, Jack Buttram, Seth Townsend, Bryan Seiders, Chuck Skypeck, Len Schaeding, and Wayne Waananen.

Thank you also to Jared Jacobs (Sundaylounge.com) for designing just about everything I do.

And to the one who matters most, with my deepest gratitude, I thank you, Sandy.

Preface

In this little book are procedures we here at Colorado Boy follow to produce our beer. Our methods have been developed over the last 20 years of brewing commercially in the seven different breweries I have owned. It's not the definitive way to brew beer. It's simply the way we do it.

It not only reflects the way I brew beer, but also it adopts some of the methods that my brewing industry peers use. That's why this book was reviewed by some of the best brewers in the U.S.—to make sure I was on the right track.

Still, much depends on the type of equipment you have in your own brewery and also on your own level of brewing expertise. Other than using nice-jacketed, glycol-cooled fermenters, much of what we do is the same as any all-grain home brewer does, only we do it bigger.

Our brewery is definitively *Frankenbrew*, reflecting the simplicity of the brewing equipment we use. It fits more in line with the start-up brewery rather than Sierra Nevada.

That being said, this book will be helpful to home breweries, aspiring commercial breweries with a limited budget, or existing breweries that would just like to see another way of doing things.

I, myself, have been brewing commercially this way since 1993 when I fashioned my first brewery out of Grundy tanks and used dairy supplies. While some of my breweries were Frankenbrew, others were really nice turnkey setups. The current breweries we operate at Colorado Boy in Ridgway and Montrose have no Frankenbrew dairy tanks in them at all; however, I wouldn't classify them as turnkey.

To aid in the instruction of many of the protocols included in this book, videos are also available on our web site, www.coloradoboy.com.

Take this all with a grain of salt. Use what you can and toss out the rest or make your own improvements. The S.O.P you develop for your own brewery could be far superior to this, and if it is, please share it with me.

Cheers,
Tom Hennessy
Ridgway, Colorado
May 2016

Keg Cleaning

Introduction

At Colorado Boy, we use only American Sankey kegs, which consist of one single entry point that has a spear going from the top to the bottom of the keg. A ball bearing is at the top, held in place with a spring. When the keg is tapped, the ball bearing is pushed down™ allowing product to exit, or in the case of cleaning, enter. This setup makes cleaning kegs very simple, as you will see.

When I first started brewing, I used to remove every spear from a keg using a keg tool that pushed the sankey fitting down, allowing me to take out a snap ring that secured the sankey fitting in place. Then, I would soak the spears in PBW. While the spears were soaking, I would put the kegs upside down with a small spray ball pointing up inside the keg, and then, using our brewing pump, recirculate the cleaning solution up inside the keg. The process was repeated in a rinse cycle, then again in a sanitize cycle. It was all very time consuming.

The current way we clean kegs is based off of commercial keg cleaning machines, albeit our own Frankenbrew version. This saves an enormous amount of time because we do not need to remove the spears, and instead use the spear as the delivery system for the cleaning solution to the keg. As long as we maintain a working pressure of 15 psi there is enough fluid force to clean the keg as well as the sankey valve and spear at the same time.

Materials and Supplies

Acid #6 (from Five Star Chemicals)
Eye protection and rubber gloves
Rubber boots
Pump
Hot hose
Spray sanitizer

Cautions

Be careful of splashing the cleaning liquid. Even diluted acid #6 can cause burns. In the event your skin is exposed, wash immediately with plenty of cold clean water.

Keg Cleaner

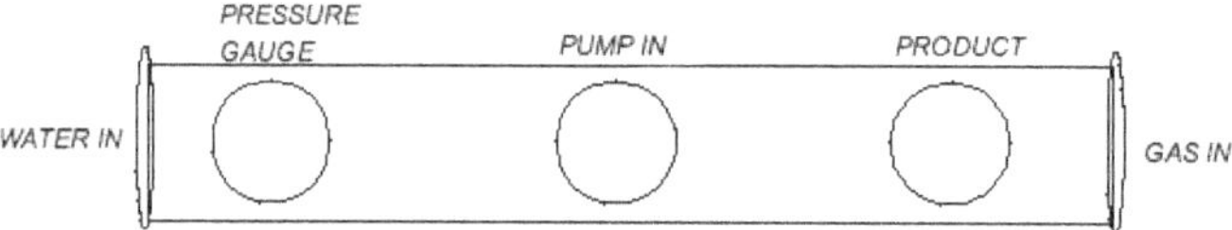

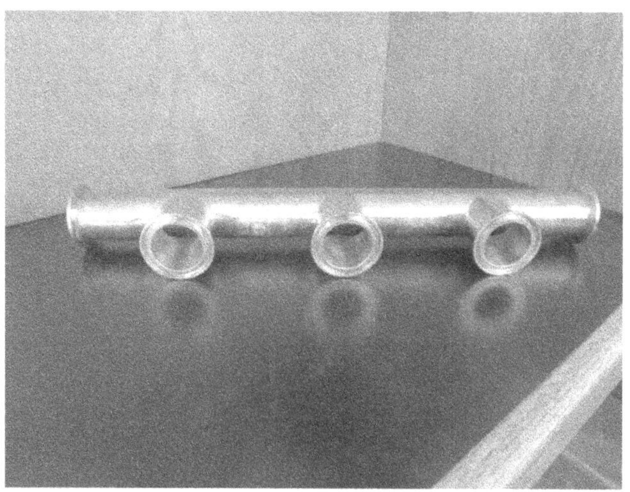

Tri Clamp Manifold

Keg Cleaning Set-up

Protocol

You will need:

1 tri-clamp (TC) manifold
1 Butterfly valve
1 Pressure gauge
1 Keg filler (see the following on how to make one)
1 Brew pump (3/4 HP)
1 Sink with a tri clamp fitting at the bottom
2 TC Elbow's
1 CO^2 to TC inlet
1 Water to TC Hose

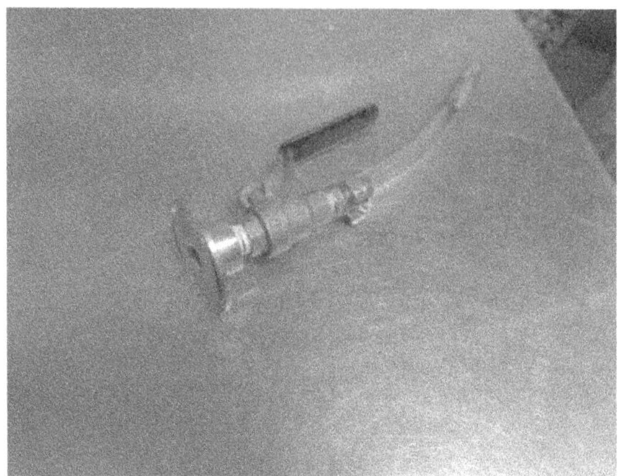

Tri Clamp to Ball Valve and CO2 Quick Connect

Tri Clamp Adapted to Hose Connection

Tri Clamp Adapter to Pressure Gauge

Butterfly Valve

Building Keg Cleaner

Before you begin, pour water on the keg sankey top to loosen any old beer that may be on the valve. This will make it easier to attach the keg cleaner.

Pour Water on Sankey to Soak Fitting

1. Attach pump outlet to middle TC, then the TC drain in the bottom of the sink attaches to the pump inlet.

Tri Clamp at Bottom of Sink

2. Attach the keg filler to the product TC.

3. Attach CO^2 to the gas inlet TC.

4. Attach a pressure gauge (e.g., a 90° TC makes the face of gauge easier to see) to the pressure gauge TC.

5. Attach a butterfly valve to the water inlet TC.

6. Attach a water hose to the butterfly valve. The butterfly valve is easier to turn on and off compared to the water valve.

Complete Keg Cleaning Set Up

Cleaning Kegs

Start by spraying down the outside of the kegs if they are unusually dirty. Use a green scrubby for tough soils.

1. Add 20 gallons hot water (140°F to 160°F) to the sink. Add the Acid #6 according to the directions on its container.

2. Tap the keg with the keg filler tube and turn upside down on the keg sink. Be sure to have the ball valves on the keg filler closed.

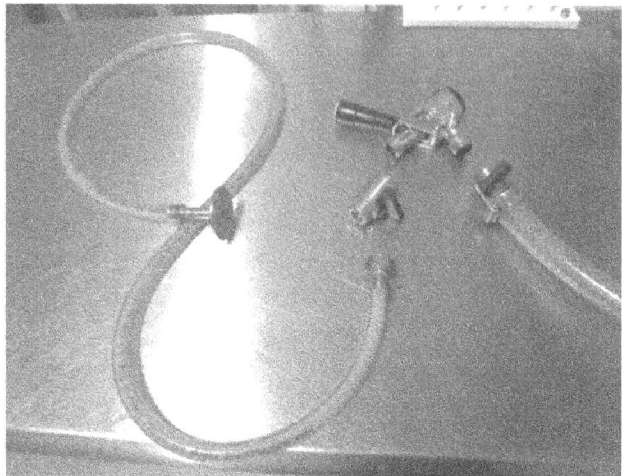

Keg Filler Parts

Keg Filler

Keg Filler attached to Keg
Notice TC on End of Product Hose

3. Run the keg filler drain hose (gas outlet) to the floor drain.

4. Open the keg filler gas outlet ball valve to drain the keg.

5. Open the keg filler product inlet ball valve.

6. Turn on the hot water to rinse the keg. Rinse twice. It helps at the end of the rinse to open up the CO^2 for a few seconds to help push out all the water.

Exhaust Tube from Keg Filler Attachment to Drain

Shut off Ball Valves

7. Replace the keg drain hose outlet back into the sink, so the product will flow into the sink rather than out to the floor drain.

8. Turn the pump on. Open the valve on the pump until you see 15 psi and run for three minutes.

9. Turn off the pump, close the pump valve, and allow acid to drain back into the sink. Push with a burst of CO^2.

CO^2 Inlet to Manifold

10. Run the keg filler drain hose back to the floor sink.

11. Turn on the hot water to rinse the keg. Rinse twice in five-second bursts. Let drain in between bursts.

Water Inlet to Manifold

12. Once all the kegs have gone through the cleaning cycle and are rinsed, drain the sink of acid #6 and rinse it out with water. Run clean water through all hoses and pump as well.

13. Add 20 gallons of non-foaming sanitizer diluted per sanitizing solution container recommendations.

14. With a clean and rinsed keg, attach the keg filler tube to the keg and turn it upside down on the sink (same as you did when you cleaned the kegs).

15. Turn the pump on and adjust the butterfly valve on the pump to 15 psi as the sanitizer moves through the keg. Remember the drain hose from the keg filler tube is feeding back into the sink, creating a loop of sanitizer solution going into the keg, then coming back out and into the sink again.

16. Set the timer to 30 seconds.

17. Turn off the pump and turn on the CO^2. This will push the remaining sanitizer out of the keg.

18. Place a hand on the ball valve on the outlet of the keg filler tube. As soon as CO^2 bubbles into the sink, indicating the keg is empty, turn the valve to the OFF position. This will allow the CO^2 to continue to flow into the keg building pressure.

19. Once the pressure reads 15 psi on the pressure gauge, turn the ball valve on the inlet portion of the keg filler to OFF. Turn off the CO^2 supply as well.

Pressure Gauge attached to Manifold

20. Take the keg off momentarily, tilt it right side up, and then back upside down again. This will allow any stray sanitizer still in the keg spear to flow out.

21. Pull the keg filler drain tube out of the sink so product can flow on the floor.

22. Open the ball valve on the outlet of the keg filler tube while the keg is still upside down and *burp* off any remaining sanitizer—just a quick "on and off" so you don't lose any pressure from the keg.

23. Turn the keg right side up, remove the keg filler, and proceed to the next keg.

24. Spray sanitizer on the sankey fitting on the clean and sanitized keg. Place a clean cap on the keg. This lets you know the keg is clean and ready to fill when you need it.

Spray Sanitizer into Sankey Fitting

Place Clean Keg Cap on Keg

Keg Cleaner Made from Keg

Our second keg cleaner we built by taking the top off an old keg and building a support on top. Kegs for cleaning go on upside-down on the support. We also added a TC on the bottom with a valve and another on the side. The manifold is attached to the supports for the upper keg. In the side is a small immersion heater from a home brew supply store that keeps the solution hot. This not only works great with kegs but also works as a grant for the mash runoff as well.

Keg Filling

Introduction

Filling kegs uses the same piece used to attach to the keg cleaner. Basically it's a sankey valve with the back flow preventers removed and ball valves that fit the beer nut threads on the sankey valve. The product side of the sankey valve has a 6' section of 5/16" braided hose with a TC on the other end. On the exhaust side of the sankey valve, a 3' section of ¾" braided hose is clamped right on the exhaust ball valve.

Filling a proper keg is all about taking your time and equalizing pressures. Since we are talking about counter pressure filling systems, you cannot just open the valves and start filling. You need to understand what is happening as you fill.

Basically, you have beer that has a desired amount of CO^2 volumes in solution, stored in a pressurized vessel, probably at about 15 psi. In order to get the beer from the pressurized vessel into your keg without the CO^2 that is already in the beer coming out, you need to match the pressure in the keg to the pressure in the tank.

Materials and Supplies

Keg Filler
Spray Sanitizer
Blank Keg Caps

Cautions

Although metal kegs are typically rated to over 40 psi, set the regulator supplying CO^2 to your keg no more than 20 psi. When pressurizing your kegs at the end of your cleaning cycle, you will only be going to 15 psi, but should you get distracted, your regulator will not let the pressure rise above 20 psi.

Most tanks are maintained at approximately 15 psi. Be careful when opening valves and especially when removing tri-clamps (TC). Going too fast could result in removing the tri-clamp from behind the butterfly valve, rather than in front of the valve, resulting in beer pouring out of the tank under pressure. Always look upstream and downstream before removing a clamp or opening or shutting a valve. Every movement has consequences!

Protocol

1. Close the ball valves on a clean and sanitized keg filler.
2. Attach keg filler to the keg.
3. Spray tank outlet with sanitizer and attach the keg filler TC to the tank racking arm.

Filling Keg from Tank

4. Open the outlet butterfly valve on the tank.

5. Slowly open the product valve on the filler. If product flows into the keg, allow time for the pressure to equalize between the tank and the keg. Do this by letting the beer go into the keg, then waiting a minute before starting to release pressure from the keg filler vent tube. Beer will stop flowing into the keg when the pressure inside the keg is the same as pressure in the tank. *If gas flows towards tank, open drain hose valve on filler to release a little gas pressure until the keg is equal to pressure in tank and beer starts flowing to keg.*

6. Adjust filler drain hose valve to allow gas to slowly bleed off. As gas bleeds off, it allows beer to flow in under equal pressure keeping CO^2 from coming out of solution and foaming.

7. When the keg is full, a little foam will come out of the filler drain. Wait until the foam turns to beer to make sure the keg is full.

8. Turn off both the filler valves and take the filler off the keg. Repeat these steps with the next keg.

9. Rinse the full keg of any spilled beer, then spray sanitizer into the keg valve, and cap.

TIP: To avoid over foaming, do not fill kegs too fast. To be sure keg is full, fill the keg on top of scale and weigh it. Total weight is dependent on the type of keg you are using.

Tank Cleaning

Introduction

Two different methods can be used in cleaning a tank.

The first method we call *nuking* a tank because we are releasing all the CO^2 inside the tank, completely emptying it, and scrubbing it clean. We also use the Nuking method for all kettles and mash tuns, as long as they have spray balls in place at the top of the tank.

Materials and Supplies

High-pressure hot water hose
PBW solution
Scrubbie and/or small brush
(To manually clean hard to reach areas)
Pump and hoses
Personal protection—safety glasses, gloves, boots

Cautions

Avoid getting PBW solution on your skin or eyes. It is a harsh cleaning agent, and if you come into contact with it, you should immediately rinse the affected area well with plenty of water.

When disconnecting any hoses or clamps, be looking upstream and downstream at what you are disconnecting to make sure there is no pressure on the clamp.

Protocol

Nuking a Tank

1. After the tank has been drained and is emptied, release all the gas to depressurize the tank. Make sure the room is well ventilated to avoid asphyxiation with CO^2. Once all the pressure is

released, open the bottom butterfly valve to drain off any leftover yeast. This will also allow CO^2 that has accumulated in the tank to vent out the bottom. Remove the racking arm, carbonating stone, and sample valve to clean separately.

2. Open the man-way and spray the tank clean. If cleaning a fermenter, use high pressure to knock off as much of the Krausen ring as possible. Use hot water! This will heat up the tank so the metal doesn't absorb the heat later from the cleaning process. Also, remove the gasket from the man-way and clean it separately in a sink to remove any yeast or hop particles from the grooves. After the gasket is cleaned, place it back on the man way door.

Spray Out Tank Using Hot Water

Remove Gasket From Man Way Door and Clean Separately

3. Attach a tri-clamp tee to the bottom outlet. On the side of the tri-clamp, attach a butterfly valve. We refer to this as the *Transfer Tee*, and it is used often in our process.

Transfer Tee

4. Close the outlet of the tank. Add 15 gallons of hot water (140°F) and 1 pint PBW through the man-way, and then close the tank.

5. Attach a hose from the bottom outlet of the transfer tee to the pump, then from the pump to the top tank spray ball.

6. Attach a small hose to the side butterfly valve on the transfer tee and run it to the drain. At this point, keep the butterfly valve closed.

Transfer Tee to Drain

7. After you have manually cleaned the sample valve and racking arm, replace them in the tank. Open the sample valve on the tank and add a butterfly valve to racking arm opening. Open this valve as well. The racking arm should be pointing in an upward direction to let PBW flow into it.

8. Start the pump slowly. As air in the tank heats up, it expands and vents out the sample valve and racking arm. It will equalize in approximately one minute. Then you can turn the pump on full, and close the butterfly valve on the racking arm, but leave the sample valve open. Let the pump run its loop for 30 minutes.

Spray Ball in Top of Tank

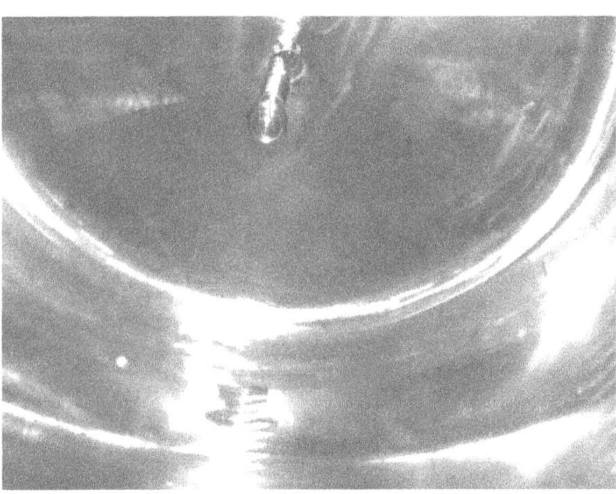
Spray Ball in Place

9. When the loop is finished, open the side butterfly valve on the transfer tee all the way, and drain the PBW out through the hose leading to the drain. Also, open the butterfly valve on the racking arm to drain the PBW that collected in it.

10. Using hot water from a holding source (mash tun, hot liquor tank, etc.), attach the hose from the pump inlet to the hot water source. You will need to place a TC blank or a butterfly valve on the transfer tee outlet so that rinse water only goes out the side to the drain. Pump the hot water through the spray ball

in a 5-sec. burst. (Make sure your butterfly valve on the racking arm is fully open.) Repeat three more times. This will rinse the tank, racking arm, sample valve, pump, and hoses at the same time.

Tri Clamp Blank Disc on Inlet of Transfer Tee

11. Open the man-way and visually inspect the tank to make sure there is no residue. Make sure also to check the sample valve and racking arm for residue as well.

Pressurized Tank Cleaning

It is possible to clean a tank that is still pressurized without opening the tank. This is especially advantageous if you are a production brewery and don't want to lose all the CO^2 that is in your 100BBL bright tank.

1. Add a tee and 90° TC with a butterfly valve pointing up after the butterfly valve on the racking arm, and close this valve.

Tee with 90° Elbow

2. Hook up a water source (I prefer the mash tun) with hot water to the CIP racking arm. The water needs to be pumped to supply enough pressure.

3. Hook a drain hose to the outlet of the tank directly to the drain. Weigh it down where it enters the drain so pressure doesn't make it pop out. A full keg works nice resting on a 90° elbow pointing into the drain.

4. This is a balancing act, but start pumping the water into the CIP arm. Wait until there is a little water in the tank, but keep an eye on your pressure gauge. You don't want to wait too long to open the bottom valve where the pressure inside the tank can build close to the tanks pressure threshold. You also don't want all the water to get out and then lose your CO^2. Leave about 15 gal. of clean water in the tank. Typically, you can start your pump, wait a few seconds, and then slowly open your bottom valve to allow the water to drain out. As long as there is water in the bottom of the tank, it will keep the CO^2 contained.

5. Once the tank has been rinsed, close the valve on the pump, and then close the valve on the CIP racking arm. Disconnect the hose from your water source that goes to the pump and connect back to the bottom of the tank you are cleaning.

6. Slowly open the valve you put on the tee and 90° TC on your racking arm. Remember, you need to have the valve to the racking arm closed so you don't release the pressure from the tank. There will be a little residual pressure in the line that will be released.

7. Add Five Star acid #6 according to the directions through the tee and 90° TC and close the valve.

Acid #6 Addition

8. Open the valve on the CIP racking arm, and turn on the pump as you open the valve on the pump. This will let the acid #6 mix with the water and begin your CIP. NOTE: you will also need to pump the rinse water, cleaner, and sanitizer through the racking arm as well.

9. After you are finished, close the pump valve and the valve at the bottom of the tank. Connect the pump to your water source, and attach a drain hose to the bottom valve of the tank.

10. Drain the acid #6 from the tank.

11. Rinse the tank as you did initially with clean water.

12. To sanitize, repeat the steps that you did with the acid #6 and drain.

At the end of this process, you should have a clean and sanitized tank that still has all of its CO^2. I think it is faster and more effective to nuke the tank each time, but the larger your tank, the more expensive the CO^2 is that you would lose by draining the tank.

If you do choose to use this system, I recommend that you go through this method with someone who has already done it a few times. Working with tanks under pressure is VERY DANGEROUS. Start with nuking your tanks until you learn more.

Carbonating Stone Cleaning and Sanitizing

Introduction

Cleaning your carbonating stone can be done while you are nuking the serving tank rather than cleaning it separately. The carbonating stone can easily clog with yeast and proteins that settle out in the beer tank, which, if not properly cleaned, can lead to infection and possible difficulty in carbonation due to blocked pores. The following protocol should be used whenever cleaning a tank.

Materials and Supplies

In addition to the basic supplies you will already be using to clean your serving vessel, you will also need a *"Y" TC with an extension on one end.* This is because the arm of the "Y" is not sufficiently long enough to contain the length of the carbonating stone. To compensate, you can use a straight piece of tri-clamp or a simple site glass.

Cautions

Cleaning the carbonating stone is done under pump pressure. Double check all connections to ensure they will not come loose during the process.

Protocol

You need the "Y" TC to attach to the outlet of your pump. On the inlet of the carbonating stone, we use a stainless steel ball valve with a gas quick connect.

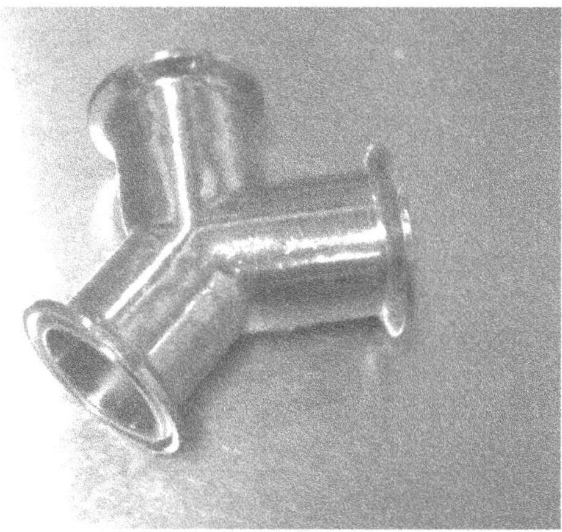

Y Tri-Clamp

This not only lets CO^2 into the carbonation stone, but also lets you bleed cleaning solution out through it as well.

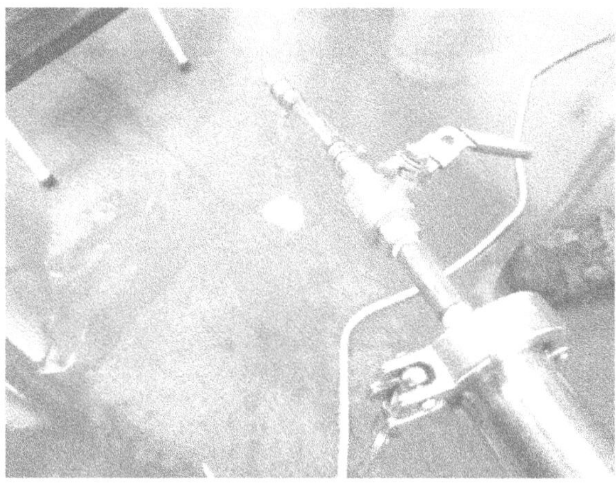

Ball Valve at Gas Inlet

Y Connection

1. Attach your carbonation stone to one side of the “Y” TC. The other side of the “Y” becomes your product outlet from the pump.

2. When you begin your cleaning loop for your serving tank, simply open the ball valve on the carbonation stone all the way to force out any yeast or sediment that may have settled into the stone. Do this until you know that the liquid is running free (3–5 sec.)

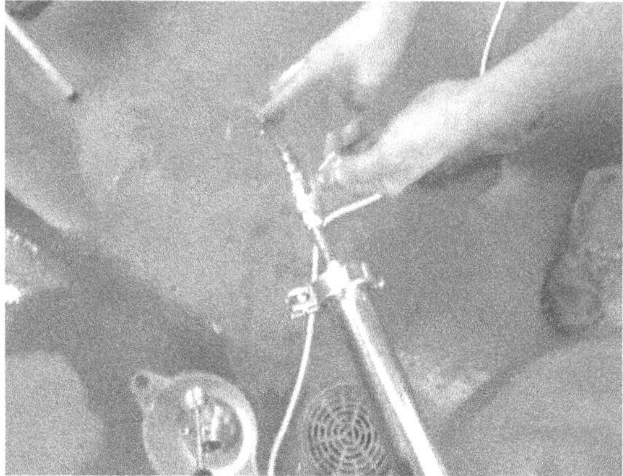

Product Purging the CO^2 Stone

3. Close down the ball valve until the cleaning solution just dribbles out, and leave it this way for the duration of the tank cleaning cycle.

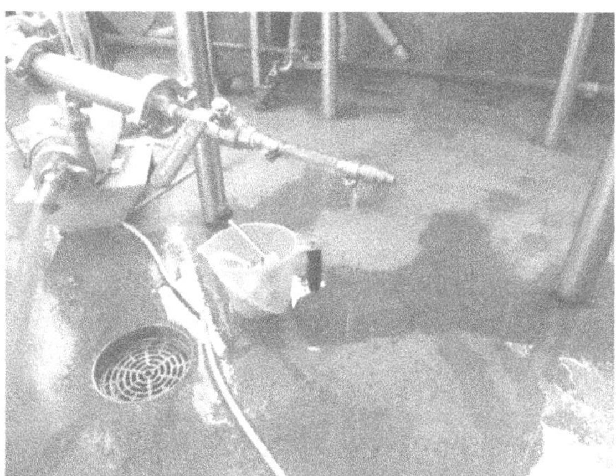

Let a Small Amount of Product Dribble out

4. When rinsing and sanitizing the stone, leave it in the "Y" assembly, and run hot water followed by sanitizer through it in the same manner described above.

After the carbonation stone has been rinsed and sanitized, you can remove it from the "Y" and place it back in the tank that it came from. Any remaining product still in the carbonating stone will be purged by connecting your CO^2 to the stone and pushing it out.

TIP: Another thing you can do to be doubly sure that your carbonation stone has been sanitized, is to wrap the stone in tin foil after you have cleaned and rinsed it. Then put the carbonation stone into an autoclave or a pressure cooker. After this, remove the tin foil and your carbonation stone will be completely sterilized.

Tank Pacification

Introduction

A CIP wash using acid #5 should be done on a regular basis to keep the inside of all the stainless steel tanks in good condition by restoring the surface to its original condition with a protective oxide film. At Colorado Boy, we do this to each tank every three months. We use a dry erase marker to write the date on each tank so we know when to schedule another pacification.

Materials and Supplies

Five Star Acid #5
Pump and hoses
Protective eyewear, gloves, and rubber boots

Cautions

Acid #5 is very dangerous if it comes into contact with skin or eyes. Therefore, it is very important to wear protective eyewear, gloves, and rubber boots. If acid should get on clothing, remove the clothing as soon as possible. If the skin should come into contact with the product, wash affected area immediately with cold water.

Five Star Acid #5

Protocol

The procedure for pacifying a tank is very similar to tank cleaning.

1. Clean and rinse a tank using the usual process.
2. Add Five Star Acid #5 in a dilution according to the instructions on the product label at 140°F to the bottom of the tank.
3. Prepare your CIP loop like you would for any tank cleaning.
4. Run the loop for 30 minutes.
5. Drain, but do not rinse the tank.
6. Rinse out hoses and pump with clean water.
7. Let the tank air dry for 24 hours.
8. After 24 hours, the tank can be sanitized and will be ready for the next use.

Tank Sanitizing

Introduction

Sanitizing a tank, which is used primarily for serving tanks and fermenters, is no different than cleaning the tank. However, methods change slightly depending on the type of sanitizer employed. Some require only a five-minute loop, while others require drying time. I recommend that you switch sanitizing solutions occasionally so that types of beer spoilers do not adapt to the same sanitizer being used.

Materials and Supplies

Transfer Hose
Pump
Sanitizer
Protective eyewear, gloves, and rubber boots

Cautions

Some sanitizers are acid-based so avoid any direct contact with skin. Sanitizing the tank involves a CIP loop, which effects pressure in the tank as air expands or contracts depending on temperature. You should always have a tri-clamp open to the tank to let the air equalize and let off any pressure that builds up with looping a hot sanitizer. Conversely, you need to be aware if the tank is hot and you loop through cold fluid, you will create a vacuum that will need to be vented as well.

Protocol

1. Add 15 gal of water (temperature is dependent on the type of sanitizer used) to the bottom of a clean and rinsed tank.

2. Add an appropriate amount of sanitizer to the water. Don't worry that it is not mixed, as it will mix during the CIP (Clean In Place) loop.

Brewer Ron Granger Adds Sanitizer

3. Attach a hose from the bottom outlet of the tank to the inlet of your pump. Then attach a hose from the outlet of the pump to the CIP inlet at the top of the tank.

4. Insert the cleaned and rinsed racking arm in its place at the side of the tank and turn it so it is pointing up. Open the butterfly valve on the racking arm all the way.

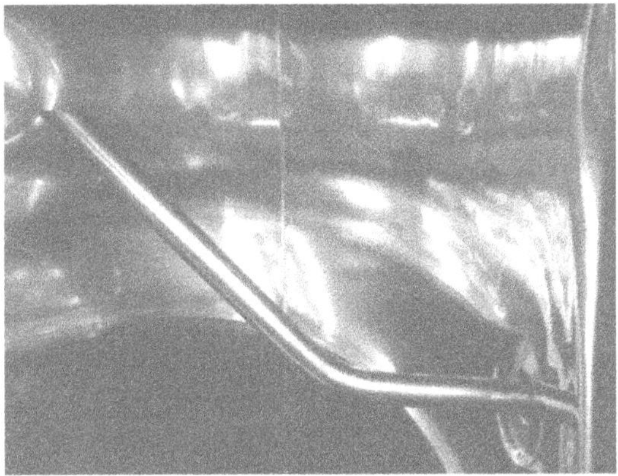

Racking Arm Pointing Up

5. Open the sample valve on the side of the tank. This is left open during the process so that sanitizer runs out the opening.

6. Start the pump and open the pump valve all the way so that it runs at full pressure.

7. Once the loop is running, close the butterfly valve on the racking arm. This will allow the arm to fill with sanitizer.

8. Run the loop as directed on the type of chemical you are using, usually from 5 to 30 minutes. If using a foaming type of sanitizer, beware that once the solution turns to foam, the pump should be turned off.

9. When finished, drain out the sanitizer. Be sure to turn the racking arm back to its DOWN position so the sanitizer will drain out of the tube. Shut the butterfly valve and sample valve.

10. Remove carbonating stone from pump "Y" set up and replace it in the side of the serving tank. Hook up CO^2 and purge out sanitizer with a short blast of CO^2. Any remnant of sanitizer in the stone will drain out the bottom of the tank. The hoses are still filled with sanitizer and will be flushed out with beer during transfer (see Beer Transfer).

Beer Transfer

Introduction

Once the beer has completed its fermentation and diacetyl rest, it is crash cooled to drop the yeast out. At this point, the beer can be transferred to a conditioning/serving tank.

At Colorado Boy, we use one tank to condition, carbonate, and serve from. The tank is not jacketed and sits in a cold room. Once the beer is ready to serve, there is a beer line that runs from the tank directly to the tap.

Materials and Supplies

- Fining agent such as Biofine Clear®
- Pump
- Transfer hose

Cautions

If CO^2 is used to push the beer to the receiving tank, make sure that the receiving tank has a top valve open so that gas can escape and not build up pressure. Also, make sure if using a pump to transfer the beer to the receiving tank, that there is an opening to the fermenter (usually just pull the blow off tube out of the blow off bucket so that a vacuum is not created in the fermenter).

Protocol

Use this method after your beer has finished fermenting, and you have chilled it and are ready for transfer.

Before you begin, make sure your receiving tank has been cleaned and sanitized. Through the top of the beer receiving tank (serving vessel, bright tank) or through the man-way, add your finings. Use

2 oz. per barrel of Biofine Clear®. This will sit at the bottom of the tank and mix with the beer as it enters.

1. With the bottom valve on the receiving tank closed and the top valve slightly open, turn on the CO^2 to the carbonating stone and allow it to run for two minutes. The CO^2 will settle to the bottom of the tank, creating a blanket against air pickup as the beer flows in. After two minutes, turn the CO^2 off.

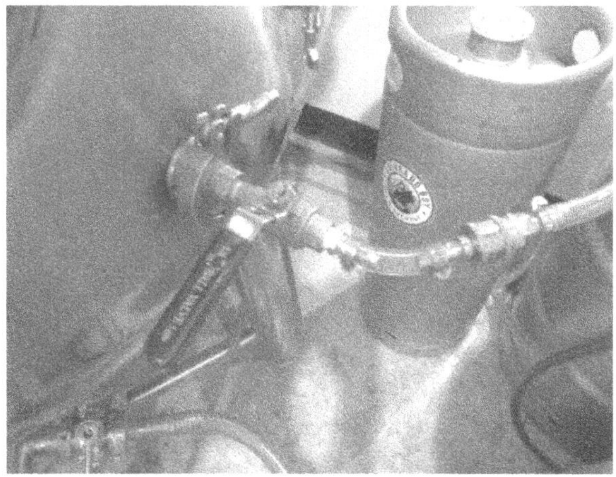

CO2 Connected to Carbonation Stone in Tank

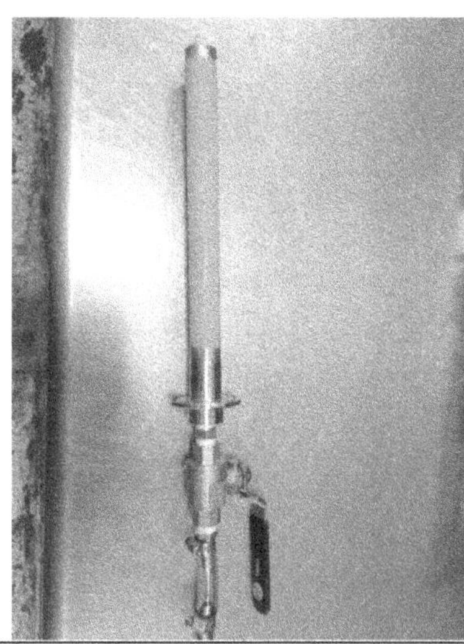

Carbonation Stone

2. Attach the long hose that was used to sanitize the serving tank to the bottom inlet of the transfer tee on the serving tank. (This was the hose used to connect to the top of the tank and comes from the outlet of the pump.)

3. The hose that came from the bottom of the serving tank connecting to the inlet of the pump now gets connected to the racking arm of the fermenter. Be sure to liberally spray the racking arm butterfly valve with sanitizer before connecting the hose. NOTE: The hose and pump should still be full of sanitizer from doing a CIP loop on the serving tank. Do not drain this sanitizer.

4. Remove the blow off tube from the blow off bucket on the fermenter to prevent a vacuum as the fermenter drains.

Remove Blow Off Tube to Avoid a Vacuum

5. All the valves should be closed. To review, the blow off tube on the fermenter is open and not in the blow off bucket. The inlet of the pump is attached to the racking arm of the fermenter. The outlet of the pump is connected to the bottom inlet of the receiving tank through the transfer tee. Start by opening the valve on the fermenters' racking arm and then, the

valve on the pump. Finally using a light (the walk in cooler can be dark), go to the transfer tee and open the valve that leads to the drain, while leaving the bottom valve to the serving tank closed. Use the flashlight to observe the sanitizer left in the hose as it moves through the hose into the transfer tee and out towards the drain. (Remember, this is done by gravity. The pump has not been turned on.) This is possible to see because the transfer hose is clear.

6. When you see solid beer coming to the transfer tee, open the bottom valve to the serving tank, and close the side valve leading to the drain at the same time. Allow the beer to flow into the tank with gravity. This will flow in smoothly and not disturb the CO^2 blanket.

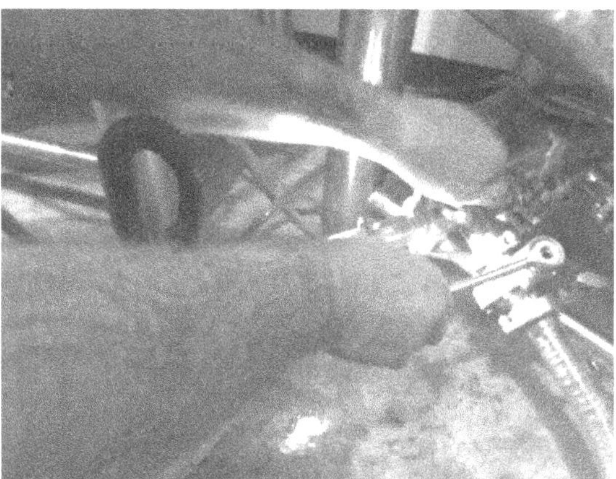

Turn off Valve to Drain and Open Valve to Tank

Use a Light to Help See When Beer Starts Flowing to Tank

7. Once the flow slows down because the two beer levels are the same in the two tanks (unless your fermenter is sufficiently high enough to gravity all the beer over), you can start the pump up slowly. Transfer the remaining beer at about the same speed that it was moving through gravity. Do this by adjusting the butterfly valve on the pump outlet.

8. If you are transferring from a conical fermenter that holds pressure, you can bypass the pump all together and hook up CO^2 to the CIP arm of the fermenter. The CO^2 pressure can push the beer from the fermenter to the serving tank.

Carbonating

Introduction

We carbonate directly in the tank we serve out of. There are three factors in carbonation: pressure, time, and temperature. Through experimentation, you can make this a repeatable process based on the size of your tank and the temperature of your cold room. The size of the tank you are carbonating and the amount of headspace in the tank are also factors that affect the time it takes to carbonate the beer. The following procedure is for the serving tanks in Montrose Colorado Boy, which hold about 195 gallons.

Materials and Supplies

Carbonating stone inserted into the side of the tank
CO^2 supply line with its own regulator
Perlick Sample Valve
Zahm-Nagel CO^2 tester

Cautions

Different tanks are rated at different pressures. Each tank should have a safety pressure relief valve that is paired with the type of tank you have. Never exceed the manufacturer's specified and tested maximum pressure.

Protocol

1. Attach CO^2 to the carbonating stone.

2. Set the regulator to 4 psi and let CO^2 into the stone for 30 min.

3. Raise CO^2 to 8 psi for another 30 min.

4. Raise CO^2 to 12 psi for another 30 min.

5. Raise CO^2 to 16 psi for another 30 min.

6. Test the carbonation with the Zahm-Nagel CO^2 tester. If not up to 2.45 volumes, then add CO^2 for 30 more min., and retest. Repeat if necessary.

7. Burp off CO^2, hook up beer gas, and bring up to serving pressure. Leaving the beer on CO^2 will over carbonate the beer.

Burping Off CO^2

8. At the end of the allotted time, attach the tri-clamp feed tube that goes to the tap.

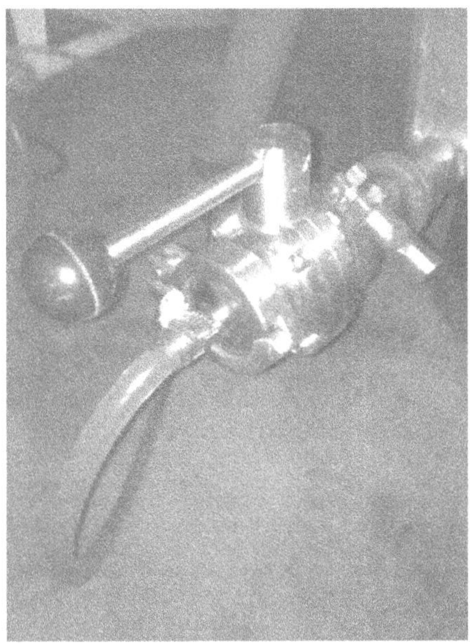

Tap Line Connected to Tank

You can check the carbonation by pouring a beer. If you get a one-finger head when pouring with the glass held up to the tap at an angle, your carbonation is perfect.

The preferred method, however, is to use a Zahm-Nagel CO^2 tester, which measures the CO^2 in solution as volumes per liter. A tester can cost approximately $1,400, but it is almost indestructible. A typical packaged beer is about 2.5 vol. We strive for about 2.45 vol., which gives enough carbonation for head retention while allowing us to fill growlers and pints without losing too much beer to excessive foaming at the tap.

Zahm-Nagel Series 1000 CO^2 Tester

Before you begin, always keep your Zahm in the cooler so that the metal gets to the same temperature as the beer you are testing. You will also need a Perlick sample valve with a lip that holds the Zahm. You can either have one permanently part of the tank or attach one to the racking arm butterfly valve.

Perlick Sample Valve

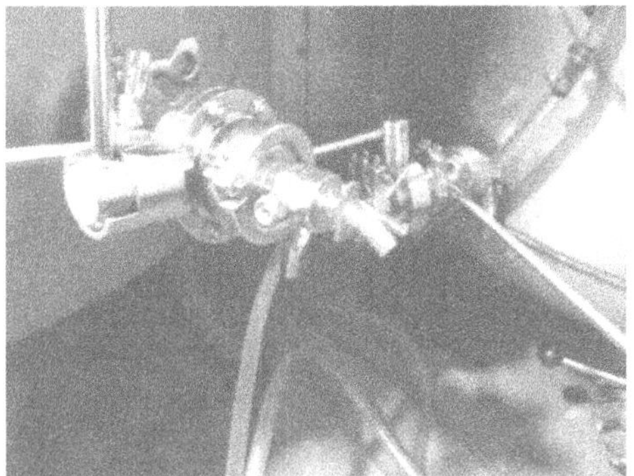

Perlick Sample Valve Attached to a Butterfly Valve

Before you take your first sample, drain some beer to clear the racking arm to avoid getting settled yeast into the Zahm.

1. With the bottom valve on the Zahm closed, use the bulb that came with the tester to pump up the pressure in the Zahm to equal tank pressure, probably about 13 to 15 psi.

2. Turn off the top valve on the tester and remove the bulb.

Bulb Unscrews from Zahm

3. Attach the tester to the Perlick sample valve securely, and open the valve.

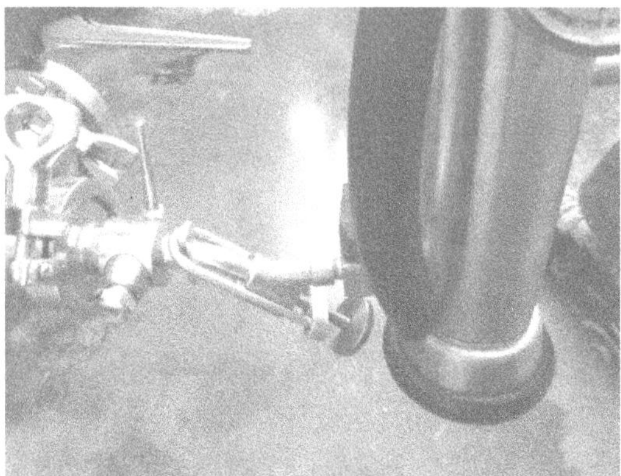

Zahm as it Attaches to Perlick Sample Valve

4. Open the bottom valve to the tester and watch the pressure reading. As beer flows into the Zahm, it will settle and equalize to that of the tank you are testing.

5. Open the top valve on the Zahm, but only slightly so that the pressure on the Zahm drops by 1 or 2 psi. This will cause beer to flow into the tester. When it fills you will see beer in the window at the top of the tester.

Beer Flowing out of Zahm and into Pitcher

6. Quickly open the valve all the way for one second to purge any bubbles from the testing chamber.

7. Shut the top and bottom valve, then the Perlick sample valve, and remove the Zahm.

8. At the bottom of the Zahm, turn the release cylinder counter clock wise to unlock it.

Locking Release Cylinder

9. Shake the tester vigorously for 30 sec. The release cylinder will drop down. Make sure you use the handles! Do not touch the Zahm body itself so as not to warm it.

10. Read the temperature and pressure, and compare them against the CO^2 volume chart provided by Zahm-Nagel.

Temperature and Pressure = Volumes CO^2

11. To clean the Zahm, open the top and bottom valves, and empty the beer out of the unit. Run hot water in the inlet, and then tip the Zahm to drain out the water. Do this three times. Push the release cylinder back up into position and lock it by turning clockwise. Leave the top and bottom valves open, and return the Zahm to the cooler so it will be cold and ready for the next use.

TIP: When beer is poured at the bar, there should be a one-finger head if the glass is held up to the tap at an angle. No beer should be spilled because of too much foam. Especially when filling growlers.

Yeast Harvesting

Introduction

We use a dry English ale strain as our house yeast. Typically we buy a pitch-able amount of yeast from www.brewingscience.com, which needs to be ordered about two weeks before it is needed. Even though we check viability of the yeast strain, it is our policy to only re-use the yeast for 10 generations. If we are brewing twice per week, that initial yeast purchase will get us through about 20 brews. By sticking to our 10-generation life cycle on the yeast, we have a greater degree of confidence that our yeast is not allowed enough time to mutate.

Following are two methods of harvesting yeast depending on the type of fermenter employed.

Materials and Supplies

- Sterile gloves
- Sterile Yeast Scoop (if not using a conical fermenter)
- Yeast Container
- Sanitized Transfer Hose (if using a conical fermenter)

Cautions

Contamination is the risk. Everything that comes into contact with the yeast must be sterile or sanitized. Avoid exposing the yeast to air as much as possible.

Protocol

Conical Fermentation Vessels

The conical fermentation tank or, *Uni-Tank*, was invented to be an all-in-one tank, that is, ferment, harvest yeast, condition, and even carbonate, all in the same tank.

Perhaps one of the biggest advantages to this type of fermenter is that it is easier to harvest the right "type" of yeast—yeast that didn't ferment too fast or too slow. This is because the yeast can settle into layers within the cone and flow out the bottom in those layers so that you can actually see the condition of the yeast.

1. Chill the finished beer enough so that the yeast will flocculate to the bottom. This usually is done over a 24-hour period.

Johnson A419 Temperature Controller

2. Sanitize a 90° TC then attach it to the bottom outlet. It is best to use an isopropyl alcohol and spray it onto the bottom valve followed by flaming it with a lighter. Just a little will do.

Spray Isopropyl Alcohol

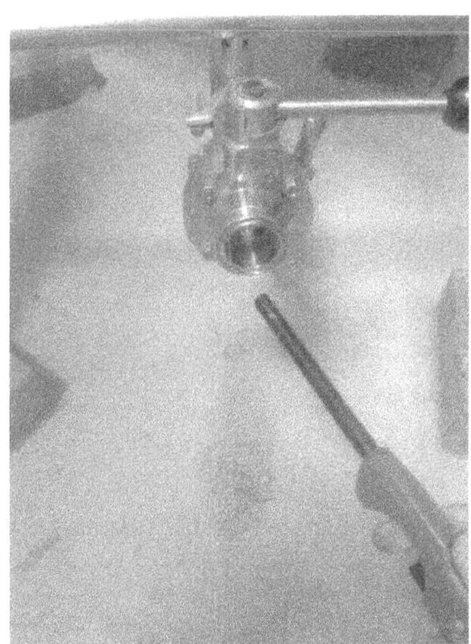

Flame to Sterilize

3. Place a container under the outlet and open the bottom valve to the fermenter. The first yeast to come out will be chunky with black material (trub) in it.

4. When the consistency of the yeast changes to a smooth custard-looking yeast (this is the middle layer), close off the bottom valve and remove the 90° tri-clamp.

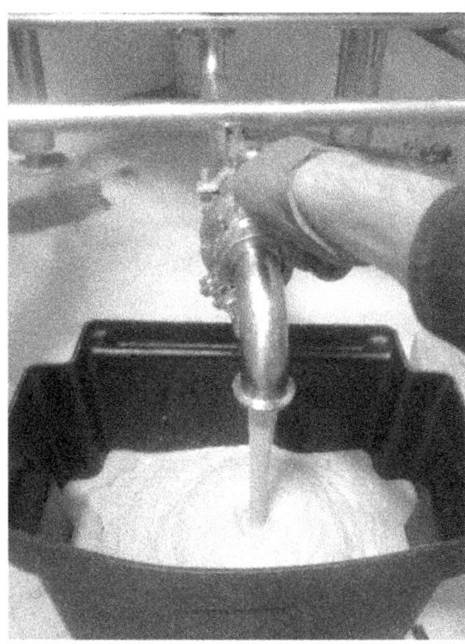

Smooth, Custard-looking Yeast, Ready to Harvest

5. Clean the bottom valve to the fermenter, and re-alcohol and flame it.

6. Connect a sanitized clear tube with a tri-clamp on one end to the bottom of the fermenter valve.

7. Connect the other end to your yeast brink or yeast container. The valve on the yeast brink should also be clean with alcohol and flamed as well.

8. Place the yeast brink on a scale, and leave an opening in the top so that air can escape during filling.

Harvesting yeast

9. Open the yeast brink bottom valve, then the bottom valve from the fermenter, and allow yeast to gravity flow into the yeast brink. Watch the weight to know how much yeast is harvesting. Leave enough head space, about 30%, so the yeast has room to expand as it sits in your cold room.

10. When a sufficient amount of yeast is harvested, disconnect yeast brink and place it in the cooler with a blow-off tube attached to the top vent, and the end of the tube into a small bucket of water with a little sanitizer in it. This allows the yeast to safely expand during storage

Yeast Brink Storage with Blow-off Tube

11. Re-attach the 90° TC to the bottom of the fermenter and collect the remaining yeast. When the viscosity is very loose, you will have gotten the majority of it.

12. Add hot water and left over sanitizing solution to the yeast to kill it, then discard it down the drain.

Dish Bottom Fermentation Vessels

At Colorado Boy in Ridgway, we use Letina white wine fermenters that are more of a dish than a cone bottom. Harvesting out of this type of a vessel is a little crude, but it works well. If you have a dairy tank type fermenter, the methods are the same.

You will need something to collect the yeast with, such as a stainless steel ladle, or a pint glass, which works well too (so long as you don't break the glass while harvesting).

1. Chill your fermenter to get the yeast to drop to the bottom.

2. Transfer the beer from the racking arm of your fermenter.

3. Spray sanitizer around the outside of the man way door and open.

4. Using your sanitized glass or ladle, remove any beer still on top of the yeast.

5. Ladle out the yeast striving for the middle section and avoid scraping yeast off the bottom. Place the yeast into your yeast pot. Harvest enough, leaving at least 30% headspace in your yeast container.

Stainless Pot as Yeast Storage

6. Store in your cooler with a blow-off tube attached to the top if using a yeast brink. You can also store your yeast in a stainless steel stockpot that you can sanitize. There is no blow-off attachment, so the excess CO^2 will just vent into the air through the loose fitting cover.

7. Add hot water and any leftover sanitizer you have to the rest of the yeast in the fermenter to kill the yeast.

8. Discard the remaining yeast down the drain.

Yeast Cell Count

Introduction

To ensure a consistent beer, pitching the proper amount of yeast for each brew can only be done by counting individual yeast cells so that we can determine the amount of yeast we have at hand as cells per milliliter.

Materials and Supplies

Microscope 400x
Hemocytometer
2 test tubes
1 ml pipet
10 ml pipet
Pipet bulb
Click counter
Distilled water
Phosphoric acid
Methylene blue

Cautions

Be consistent and precise with measurements and methods for counting yeast to ensure consistency in results. Do not take any shortcuts.

When harvesting yeast, take a sample of the yeast you are about to save and set is aside so you can do your cell counts and viability.

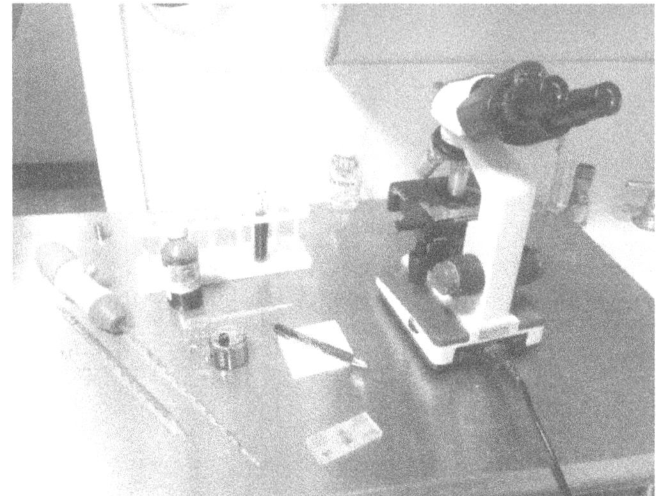

Yeast Cell Count Set-up

Protocol

To begin fill two test tubes with 9 ml of distilled water using a 10 ml pipet.

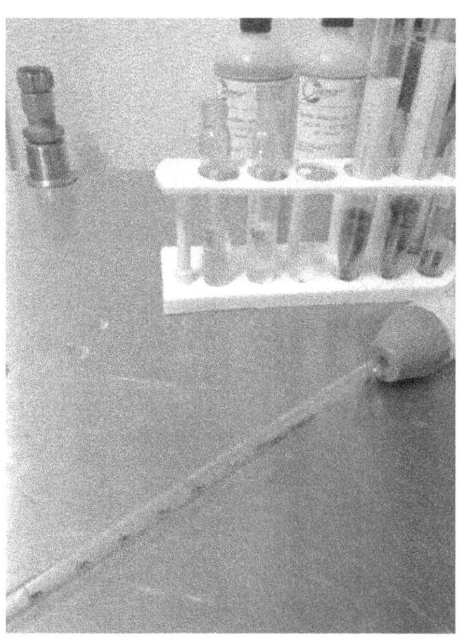

2 Test Tubes with 9 ml of Distilled Water in Each

1. Draw 1 ml of the set aside yeast and place it in the first test tube. This gives you a dilution rate of 10:1. If the yeast is forming clumps, add one or two drops of phosphoric acid to the test tube and shake. This breaks up the flocs and gives a more uniform count.

2. Now take 1 ml out of the first test tube and add it to the 9 ml of water in the second test tube. This will give you a 100:1.

3. Add enough Methylene Blue (about 0.5 ml) to the second test tube so that the solution turns cobalt blue and shake.

4. Place a sample of this solution on the hemocytometer with a cover slip. Place this on the microscope.

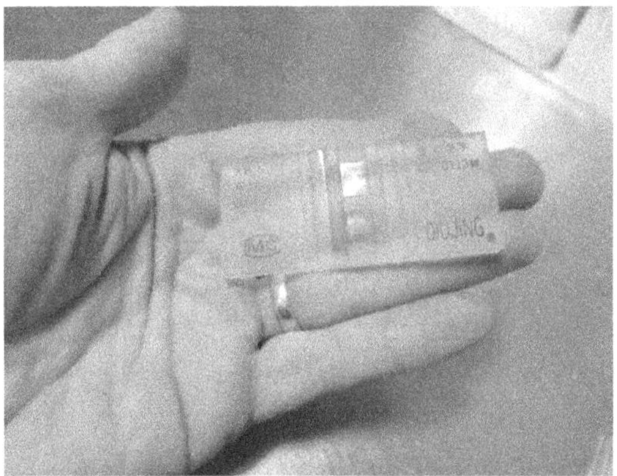

Hemocytometer

5. There are 25 squares each containing 16 smaller squares on the slide. The 16 smaller squares have three lines bordering them. Rather than counting all of the large 25 squares, count only the squares in the four corners and the one in the center of the 25.

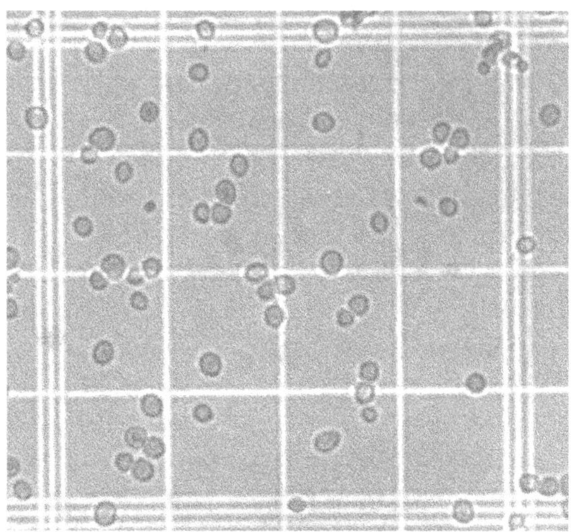

One of 25 Grids with 16 Squares
(Photo credit: Brewing Science Institute)

6. Only count cells that do not touch the top or left lines. It is ok if they touch the bottom or right lines of the triple lines that surround the 16 squares. If a cell has a smaller cell touching it, count that as two, as long as the smaller cell is at least half the size of the larger cell.

7. Begin counting cells including any that are blue in all 16 squares. Once you have a count, go back and count only the blue ones. When you are finished, you should have a count that looks something like this: 74/3. In other words 74 cells, three of which are blue

8. Continue to count all four corners and the middle group. When you are done total everything up. It should look like 382/13.

9. Divide the number of blue cells by total to find percentage of dead cells. Yeast is viable with a minimum of 90% live cells.

10. Multiply the total cells counted in the five squares by 50,000 to account for the squares not counted. Multiply this number by your dilution factor (which was 100:1) or just add two extra 0s. Your total will look something like 1,910,000,000 (382 x 50,000 x 100). This is how many cells you have per ml.

11. Assuming you are brewing a 15°P ale and that you need one million cells per ml per °P, then multiply your 1,910,000,000 cells by 15 million. Then you need to step it up from ml to gallons to get your pitch rate in volumes. The easiest way to do this entire calculation is to go to www.brewingscience.com and use their pitching rate calculator.

12. Write down your viability and cell count on a sticky note and attach it to your yeast brink so you know how much yeast you have for your next brew.

Yeast Pitching: Closed Method

Introduction

This method allows you to introduce your yeast without exposing the yeast to air. It also gets the yeast mixed in with the oxygen rich wort in a complete way. This is the preferred method at Colorado Boy.

Materials and Supplies

Yeast Brink
Digital Scale
Sanitized hose

Cautions

Be careful to sanitize and/or sterilize all connections before introducing yeast.

Protocol

1. Calculate how much yeast is needed for your brew. You can calculate the volume using the Pitching Rate Calculator provided on www.brewingscience.com.

2. To convert liquid pints of yeast into weight, divide the amount of pints required by 1.2. This accounts for the different density of yeast. For example, 8½ pints of yeast is 7.08 pounds.

3. Use the transfer tee that goes to the bottom of your fermenter. This tee is used to flush out sanitizer when transferring wort to the fermenter. The heat exchanger is packed with sanitizer so this goes through the transfer tee to the drain. Once the wort is visible to the tee, the valve to the drain is turned off and the valve to the fermenter is opened. This drain part of the tee gets sterilized with alcohol and flame before a sanitized hose is attached from the transfer tee to the yeast brink.

4. Place the yeast brink on a scale. The best scales have a separate read out so the yeast brink doesn't obscure the numbers. Zero out the scale.

5. Attach CO^2 to the top of the yeast brink to pressurize it.

6. Open the bottom valve of the yeast brink. The yeast won't go anywhere because you still have the valve on the other end of the hose closed.

7. Once you are satisfied that the wort is transferring at the proper temperature, open the valve on the tee where the line goes into the wort transfer hose just part way so the yeast transfers as slowly as possible. Keep an eye on the weight until it reaches the amount based on your calculations. Be sure to account for the weight of the yeast in the hose as well.

Yeast Brink to Transfer Tee

Yeast Pitching: Open Method

Introduction

If you do not have a yeast brink, and instead are using an open yeast container such as a stainless pot, this method is simple and works great.

Materials and Supplies

Yeast Pot
Ladle or pint glass

Cautions

If using a pint glass, be extremely careful that you do not hit the side of the fermenter when adding yeast. A broken glass in your yeast will lead to a bad day.

Protocol

1. Determine the amount of yeast needed based on the same calculations in the previous chapter (see Yeast Pitching—Closed Method); however, there is no need to convert to weight as you will be pitching yeast by volume.

2. Skim off any beer that has floated to the top of your yeast pot.

3. Before you transfer your wort at the end of your brew, spray the man-way door of your fermenter with sanitizer, and open. If using a dairy tank fermenter, simply open the top.

4. With a sanitized ladle or pint glass (be careful not to break the glass on the side of the opening), scoop out the appropriate amount of yeast and add it to the fermenter.

5. Re-spray the man-way door with sanitizer and close it up. The yeast will blend with the wort as it flows into the fermentation tank.

Brewer Elliott Bell Ladles Yeast into a Letina Fermenter

Brew Prep

Introduction

At Colorado Boy, we brew prep the day before a brew to save time on brew day. Based on the way we brew, all hot liquor is made with the kettle; therefore, it is faster if we heat the water the day before so it will be ready for strike the next morning.

Materials and Supplies

Same equipment used for brew day.

Cautions

Make sure that all sanitized parts (heat exchanger, hoses, and fermenter) are closed up at the end of brew prep so as not to risk infection from air.

Protocol

Start by filling the kettle with cold water and turning on the kettle. Our water has chlorine in it so getting it to almost a boil the day before cooks off the chlorine. If you have Chloramine in your water, you will need to filter it.

1. Clean and rinse the empty fermenter according to tank cleaning protocol. Be sure to take the gasket off the door and thoroughly clean it as well.

2. Use hot water pumped to supply sufficient pressure to the heat exchanger to rinse out the PBW left packed in from the last brew (the mash tun is a good holding tank to pump from). When pumping the hot water through the heat exchanger, open and close the butterfly valve on the product exit of the heat exchanger that the water is running through. Only close the valve for less than a second and open again. Repeat this

four or five times. The buildup of pressure helps to rinse in between the plates.

3. Add 15 gal of sanitizer to the fermenter and close man-way. Turn racking arm pointing up and open butterfly valve on it. Also open the sample port.

4. Attach oxygenating stone up to heat exchanger product outlet.

O^2 Stone Set Up to the Outlet of the Heat Exchanger

5. Attach a hose from the bottom of the fermenter to the pump inlet.

6. Attach a hose from the pump outlet to the heat exchanger product inlet.

7. Attach a hose from the oxygenating stone outlet to the top of fermenter spray ball.

8. Open the pump valve to let sanitizer in to prime, then slightly close it off to start pump. As product starts to move through system, open the pump up all the way.

9. When all the air pressure has equalized in the tank, close off the butterfly valve on the fermenter's racking arm. This will gradually fill with sanitizer.

10. Slightly open up the valve on the oxygenating stone gas inlet to let sanitizer dribble out.

Sanitizer Running through O^2 Stone

11. Run through the sanitation cycle.

12. Turn off the pump. Turn off the two valves on the heat exchanger for the inlet and outlet. Then take the hoses off the heat exchanger and on the outlet to the oxygenating stone. Put on a tri clamp blank disk to keep the sanitizer in the stone. Take the hose from the outlet of the pump and hook it up to the hose end that came off the oxygenating stone. This will leave the sanitizer in the hoses you will be using the next day for wort transfer, and it seals up the hoses.

13. Weigh out your grain and place the bags in the brew house. This is especially important in the winter months so the grain can reach room temperature and will not cool down the mash.

Grain Weighed Out and Ready for Milling

14. Turn off kettle around 195°F. If possible, close off steam vent from outside to prevent cold air getting into kettle during the night, which would cool the water too much (worth the effort). The next morning, the water should be around 166°F. Turn on the kettle to bring it up to a strike temperature of 169°F (which when mashed in will produce a mash temperature of about 153°F). Note these temperatures could change depending on recipe formulations.

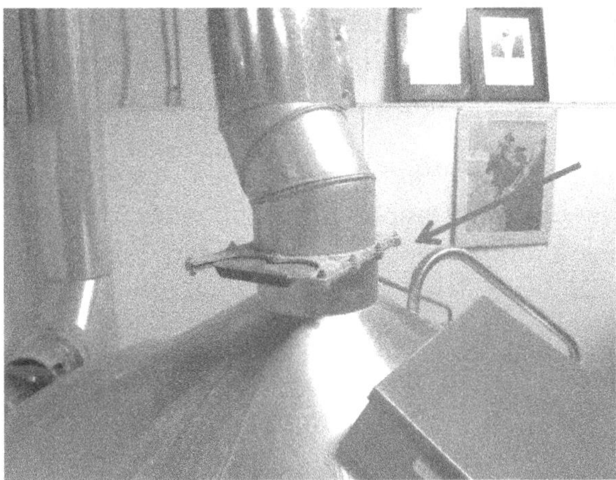

Steam Vent Shut-off

Brew Day

Introduction

Colorado Boy does not have a turnkey brewing system. Our way of brewing, however, is simple and allows for any combination of tanks to be employed, which is the main reason our brewing systems are less expensive. A typical Colorado Boy 7 BBL system should cost less than $60,000 new. The following is a step-by-step process of how our brew day goes.

Materials and Supplies

- Brewers boots
- Rubber gloves
- Eye protection

Cautions

Scalding from hot wort is a serious threat so attention needs to be placed on boil overs and disconnecting hot hoses. Always look upstream and downstream when disconnecting hoses, and be aware of any built up pressure on the hose from the pump.

Lifting bags of grain and spent grain can cause strain to the back. Proper body mechanics (e.g., not lifting too much at one time) needs to be observed.

Protocol

Turn on the kettle to bring the strike water up to temp.

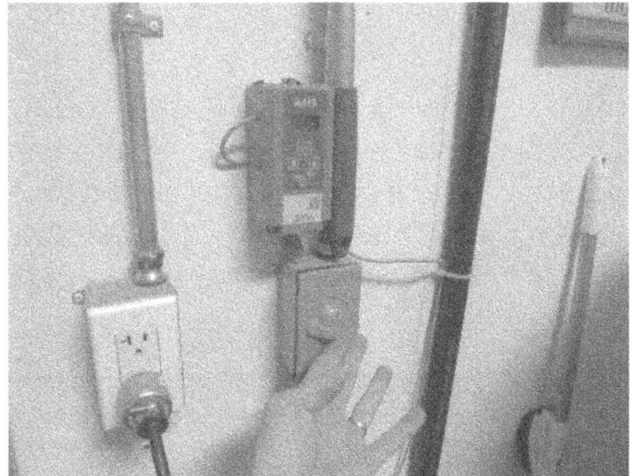

Power Switch Turns on Burner Controller

1. Measure out phosphoric acid and add to the kettle.

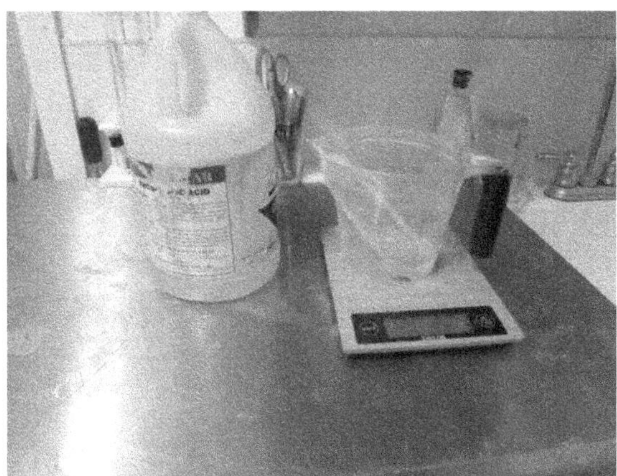

Weigh Acid Additions for Accuracy

2. Measure out calcium additions and set next to the mash tun.

Gypsum Mixed with Hot Water

3. Add one bag of grain to the mill hopper with the chute closed.
4. Whirlpool the kettle to mix acid addition to the water.
5. Connect water from the kettle to pump to the grist hydrator.
6. Set up sight tube on the kettle to measure water volume.

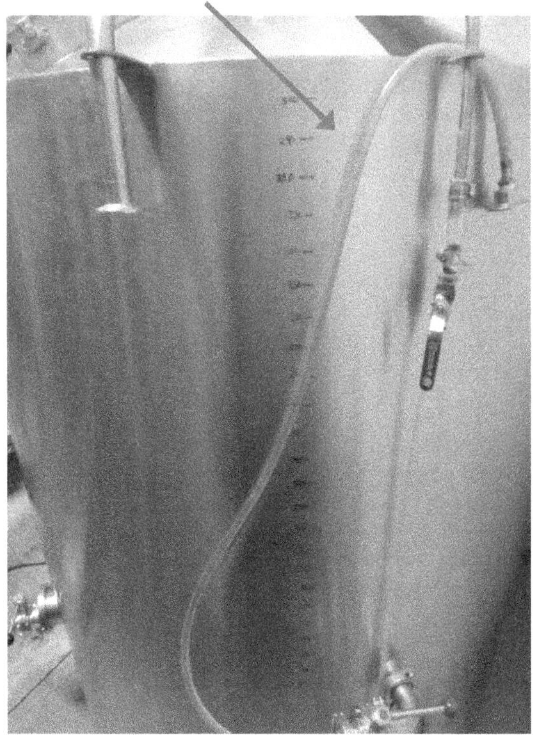

Site Tube Showing Water Level

7. Calculate how much water for strike to mash tun.

8. Start pumping water to the mash tun through the grist hydrator, enough to fill the space below the screens but not so much to go over the screens.

9. Start the auger.

10. Start the mill and slowly open the chute at bottom of the mill hopper. Keep an eye on the mill during mash in to keep grain going in consistently until all the grain is used.

Hydrated Mash Entering Tun

11. During mash in, use a paddle to break up any dough balls.

12. At the end of mash in, set the timer for 30 min.

13. Take the temperature and pH of the mash, and the close lid.

Brewer Steve Wood Taking pH Reading

14. Turn on the kettle again to heat the remaining water to 180°F for sparge.

15. Set up the pump to transfer the kettle water to the hot liquor tank and transfer the water.

16. Set up the grant below the mash tun with a strainer in the grant to catch any grain particles. Make sure the strainer is below the liquid level to avoid any hot side aeration.

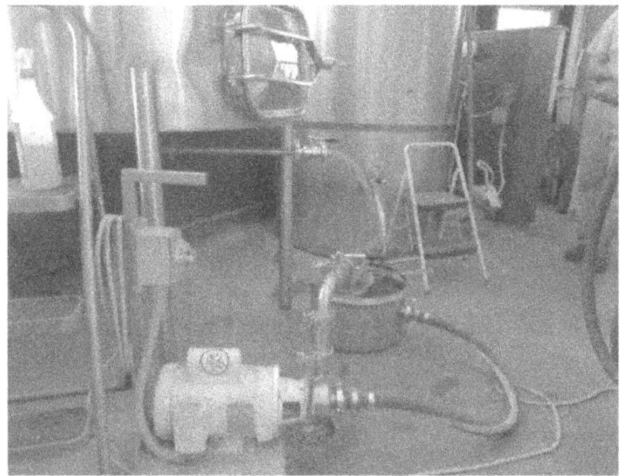

Grant Set-up

17. Set up to pump from the grant to the vorlauf set up on the mash tun.

18. Start the vorlauf and run for 10 min. or until the wort is clear. There should be 5 ml or less of grain particles per 1,000 ml of wort.

19. Attach a hose from the hot liquor tank to the sparge arm on the mash tun.

20. Start pumping wort from the grant to the kettle slowly.

21. Start the sparge. Establish and maintain 1" of water above grain bed.

Maintain 1 in. Sparge Water on top of Grain Bed

22. Transfer the wort to the kettle. Timing should be 75 min.

23. Take a gravity reading of last running's of the wort from the mash tun.

24. Take an initial gravity of the kettle wort and compare to target on your brew log.

Copper Pipe for Hydrometer Flask

25. Clean the mash tun.

Mash Door Height Just above Standard Trash Can

26. When the wort begins to boil set the timer for 30 min. to remind you about the first hop addition.

27. Add 1 oz. of Fermcap® to kettle.

Fermcap®

28. Add hops according to recipe schedule. Use the timer to count down to the next addition.

Mark Buckets to Keep Hop Additions Correct

Add First Hops Slowly to Avoid Boil Over

29. Add yeast to the fermenter (if using open pot method).

30. Set up for wort transfer—heat exchanger, O^2 set up.

O^2 Set-up coming off Outlet of Heat Exchanger

31. Fifteen minute before the boil ends add kettle finings.

Kettle Finings Addition

32. Set up for whirl pool (pump out of bottom and back into whirl pool inlet on kettle).

33. Turn the kettle off and whirlpool for 10 min.

34. Add hops to the whirlpool if the recipe calls for it.

35. Turn the whirlpool off and let it rest for 10 min.

36. Connect the outlet of the pump to the heat exchanger.

37. Take a final volume reading from the kettle.

Final Kettle Volume Taken from Site Tube

38. Take a final gravity reading of the wort.

39. Open the transfer tee on the fermenter to the drain. The fermenter valve stays closed.

Transfer Tee

40. Hook up O^2 to the inline oxygen infuser.

41. Start cold water to the heat exchanger.

42. Check that all valves are open except for pump valve.

43. Start the pump and slowly open the valve till wort flows. You will see movement through the clear transfer hose you use after the heat exchanger.

44. Follow wort to the transfer tee, then close valve to the drain and open the valve to the fermenter.

45. Once flow has stabilized to desired temp, start the O^2 flow in the oxygen infuser.

46. Add yeast (if using closed method).

47. At the end of transfer, turn the pump off. Connect the kettle outlet hose to CO^2 and push the last wort through system.

48. Record the transfer time.

End of Brew (Clean)

Introduction

Not only do we clean everything from the brew, but also we want to leave everything ready for the next brew. We feel it is important to leave the tanks polished and floors cleaned as customers are always looking at the brewery. A clean brewery is a sign of professionalism.

Materials and Supplies

Boots, Eye Protection, Gloves
PBW
Scrubbies
Squeegee

Cautions

Cleaning is a wet environment, which can cause slips and tripping over hoses that are a tangle everywhere after a brew. Do the cleaning systematically, one step at a time, so that you always know where you are in the process.

Protocol

Cleaning the brew house after a brew is simple by flowing water, then PBW, through all your systems but in reverse. During wort runoff, you were recapturing your heat exchanger water in your clean mash tun, which should be between140°F and 150°F. Now use this water to do your cleaning, thereby not wasting the BTUs you generated during your brew.

1. Attach the hose that went from your kettle to the pump inlet, to the mash tun that contains the hot water leftover from your recapture from the heat exchanger.

2. Open the valves, and pump a decent amount of this water through all the hoses, heat exchanger, and O^2 stone.

3. Attach a drain hose to the bottom of the kettle, and spray the kettle out as best you can of hops and trub.

Drain from Kettle

4. Transfer about 20 gal. of hot water to the kettle, and add an appropriate amount of PBW.

5. Reverse the direction of your hoses so that your cleaner comes i) out of your kettle to the pump, ii) out of the pump into the O^2 stone, iii) into the heat exchanger the opposite way, and iv) through to the spray ball at the top of your kettle. Start this CIP loop and let it run for 30 min.

6. Open up all the way the O^2 inlet on the oxygenating stone set up first to purge any hop residue that might be stuck in it. Then reduce the flow to a trickle, the same way you sanitized it. Keep this going the entire length of your CIP run.

7. With five minutes left in the CIP, turn everything off, redirect the hose that was attached to the spray ball, and attach it to the whirlpool arm. Turn the pump back on, and run for the last five minutes to gain contact time with cleaner in the hard-to-reach areas of the whirlpool arm.

8. At the end of the CIP, pack the heat exchanger (See next chapter).

9. Drain the kettle. Using a long brush, reach down into the kettle from the man-way and scrub any stubborn dirty areas.

10. Re-attach pump to mash tun where you still have leftover hot water. The drain from the kettle is still open. With heat exchanger now out of the loop, pump clean hot water through everything to the spray ball of the kettle and let drain. Remember to run hot water through the whirlpool arm and any other areas that were in contact with cleaner.

11. Disconnect and store all hoses and parts. Completely drain the kettle and leave the man-way door open.

12. Any spare parts that were not part of the loop, including extra gaskets and tri-clamps, put into a PBW soak bucket.

13. Dismantle pump head and clean.

5 Minutes Cleaning Pump Seals

14. Polish tanks, spray floor down, and squeegee dry.

15. Have a beer!

Packing the Heat Exchanger

Introduction

The heat exchanger is one of the most likely places where beer can become infected because of all its many nooks and crannies where bacteria can form. This method of "packing" the heat exchanger will clean out those small places, and it is easy to do! This process occurs at the end of your CIP loop cleaning the kettle, heat exchanger, and oxygen stone

Materials and Supplies

Pump
Hoses
PBW

Cautions

Packing the heat exchanger means packing it under pressure. We only want a slight increase in pressure when packing to open the plates slightly. Too much pressure could blow a plate gasket. Do not over pressurize!

Protocol

1. While at the heat exchanger as you are running your cleaning loop with the pump on full, close off the outlet valve on the heat exchanger and count to two seconds.

2. Next close off the inlet to the heat exchanger.

3. Immediately close off the pump valve and turn the pump off. This whole process shouldn't take more than three seconds.

4. Once you have the pump turned off, open the outlet valve on the pump so that any pressure that built up in the hoses is released back into the kettle. Be very careful when taking apart hoses that may still have pressure in them.

Now that the pump is shut off, as well as the heat exchanger valves in and out, you can disconnect the heat exchanger from the CIP loop. It will remain packed with hot PBW under pressure until you need it again for your next brew. At that time, you will open it up and thoroughly wash it out with hot clean water.

Because it is "packed" under pressure with hot PBW, all the plates get thoroughly soaked in the cleaning solution. This is the most effective method for getting a cleaning agent into all the surface areas and getting them really clean.

Line Cleaning

Introduction

No matter what care we take and how good our recipes are, if the beer lines aren't clean, the beer will taste *off*. This is particularly important when customers bring in their own kegs to be filled and then poured on their personal Kegerator. In such instances, your customers might be at someone's house drinking your beer, blaming you for the beer not tasting right. When a customer takes a keg, we review this process with them, and we even may lend them our line cleaning set up.

At the pub we have it on our schedule to clean lines every other Monday.

Materials and Supplies

Keg cleaning tank.
PBW or Acid #6 for the lines (either can be used)
Tap wrench
Tap brush

Cautions

There is usually residual pressure in the lines, so that even if you un-tap a keg, you should open the tap on that line to release any line pressure before you pull the tap off for cleaning.

Protocol

1. Prepare a hot PBW solution (140°F) in a 5-gallon keg. Make sure it is mixed well. We use a twist off Sankey valve so it is easy to put solution in it. You could also use a 2½ gallon line cleaning set up that Foxx Equipment sells. It has a Sankey valve that unscrews as well.

2. Attach cleaning solution keg to a Sankey tap and run through the beer line. When the beer comes out of the tap, it will be followed with the hot PBW solution. Discard the beer, but save the PBW into a pitcher. Run enough to almost fill the pitcher.

3. Detach the Sankey and proceed to the next tap repeating the process.

4. When all the beer lines are full of clear PBW (no traces of beer left in them) and the Sankey taps are disconnected, remove the valve taps from their shanks. This is done with a tap wrench turning clockwise to remove.

5. Place the tap faucets in the pitchers in the open position so the taps can soak.

6. With a tap brush dipped into the PBW solution from the pitcher, scrub out the shank.

Scrubbing out Tap Shank

7. Inspect the tap faucet gaskets, replacing if necessary, and then put the tap back on the shank.

8. Use the tap brush to clean the inside of the tap itself.

9. Replace the PBW in the keg with hot clean water.

10. Flush all the taps out with at least one pitcher (64 oz.) of water.

11. Hook the beer back up and pour out one pint.

Cleaning Beer Engine

Introduction

Beer engines have a pump cylinder inside them that holds 5–10 oz. of beer. Unless the beer engine has a jacket, the beer inside the cylinder is at room temperature and can spoil faster than cold beer. Therefore, it is important that the beer engine is cleaned more frequently.

Materials and Supplies

Pitcher
Cleaning solution—PBW, Acid #6
Rubber Gloves and eye protection

Cautions

Cleaning solutions such as PBW or Acid #6 are corrosive on skin. If any skin comes into contact through splashing or drips, immediately wash the affected area with plenty of cold water.

Protocol

Nightly

1. Un-tap the beer engine and place tap into a pitcher of hot water.

2. Pump the water through the beer engine by pulling the beer engine handle. Leave enough water in the beer line so it can soak overnight. Caution: If you are running a glycol trunk line, do not leave water in the line or it will freeze.

Pull One Pitcher of Hot Water through Beer Engine

3. At the beginning of the next shift, re-tap beer and pull through one pint to get all the water out.

Weekly

1. Un-tap the beer engine and place tap into a pitcher of PBW around 140°F.

2. Pump the PBW or Acid #6 through the beer engine as you did with water, and let the last of it sit in the line for one hour to soak.

3. Pump through one pitcher of hot water to rinse out all cleaning solution.

4. Pump one pint of beer through the line to rinse out the water.

Cask Ale

Introduction

We use two separate methods for making cask ale. The first is for traditional firkins that will either be tapped at the bar with a spigot or pulled through a beer engine without a sparkler attached to the wand of the beer engine. Because the casks are primed, there is sufficient carbonation to achieve a solid head on the beer without the use of the sparkler.

Living in Colorado where it is dry and hot a good portion of the year, we serve our cask-conditioned ales at cooler beer temperatures. We call this American Cask Ale.

Materials and Supplies

- Erlenmeyer flask
- Rubber Gloves
- Mallet for hammering in bung

Cautions

Actively fermenting beer is being added to your cask so make sure you are extremely careful to keep the area where you are working dust-free and as clean as possible.

Protocol

Method One

1. Start with a clean and sanitized Firkin or Pin.

2. If dry-hopping or adding any other flavors, add them at this time through the bung.

3. Add 180 ml of actively fermenting beer to a Pin or 400 ml to a Firkin. You can get this beer from another beer that is fermenting or you can save some wort from a previous brew and add yeast, shake and let sit for six hours until it is at an active fermentation state.

4. With a sanitized hose, gravity fill the cask from the finished beer in the fermenter until about 90% full through the bung. Keep a small sheet of foil over the opening while you are filling since the hose you are using to fill is smaller than the bung.

Use a Piece of Foil to Help Cover Bung Opening When Filling

5. Add an appropriate amount of finings to the cask, and hammer the bung into place.

6. Roll the cask around a bit to mix up all the beer, yeast, and finings.

7. Set cask in a cool part of the brewery where the temperature is ±65°F to condition for one to two weeks.

8. 24 hours prior to tapping, chill the cask on its side at cold beer temperature, or at cellar temperature depending on brewer's preference

9. To tap, hammer in a spile in the top of the bung to release built-up pressure. Pull the spile out or leave in loose so that a vacuum isn't created when beer is dispensed and so that the beer can flow.

10. Tap the spigot into the keystone in the front and serve, or attach the spigot to your beer engine to serve.

Method Two

After doing the following method for some time, I traveled to the UK to see how larger breweries were preparing their casks. I discovered they were doing it the same way. This is a simple way to serve cask ale that pours a perfect pint through a beer engine every time.

1. Ferment your beer the normal way, chill and transfer to a conditioning/serving tank.

2. Allow the beer to condition out for at least a week. You can dry hop in the conditioning tank as well.

3. Before you carbonate your tank, rack the finished beer into your cask. You can fine it in the cask or fine it in the conditioning/serving tank.

4. Let the beer condition further in the cask.

5. Tap the cask to the beer engine.

Since the beer has already been conditioned and fined in the larger tank, a sankey keg can be used as your cask. With this method, you want a sparkler on your beer engine. By pulling a pint with a little force, you get a nice cascading foam that sets up to a perfect creamy head on clear beer every time.

Dry Hopping

Introduction

We utilize two different methods for dry hopping based on the two types of fermenters used in both Colorado Boy locations.

Ridgway uses two Letina white wine fermenters that are not conical. Because there is no way to harvest yeast from these without first removing the beer, we dry hop in the serving tanks.

Montrose has two conical fermenters, which allow us to pull the yeast off at the end of fermentation and then dry hop right in the fermenter.

Method One – Serving Tank Dry Hop

Materials and Supplies

Poly paint straining bag from hardware store
String
Spray sanitizer
Rubber gloves

Cautions

When positioning the hop bag in the serving tank, make sure that it cannot get in the way of the racking arm and clog it.

Protocol

1. Soak in sanitizing solution a poly paint straining bag and synthetic string,

2. Weigh out hops.

3. Remove bag and string from sanitizing solution, shake excess sanitizer from them, fill with hops, and tie the bag closed with the string. Leave enough room in the bag so that the hops can swell when wet and still have room to move in the beer that saturates the bag.

4. Tie the bag to either the carbonating stone or the racking arm. Tie it so it can move around a bit but not enough to clog the racking arm.

5. Proceed to transfer beer to the tank as normal.

Setting Hop Bag in Tank Tied to Racking Arm

Method Two – Dry Hopping in Fermenter

Materials and Supplies

Rubber gloves
Spray sanitizer

Caution

If the opening at the top of the fermenter is small, use a funnel.

Protocol

1. After the diacetyl rest at the end of fermentation, reduce temperature on fermenter to 64°F and let sit for 24 hours.

2. Harvest yeast off bottom of fermenter.

3. Add hops in loose through an opening at the top, spraying area liberally with sanitizer before opening. Add hops slowly.

4. Close up the top again.

5. Turn fermenter temperature back up to 70°F and let hops remain in fermenter for at least five days.

6. Crash cool fermenter and transfer as usual.

Colorado Boy Ridgway & Montrose

In order to put things in perspective when looking at our SOPs, it might be helpful to understand what type of brewery Colorado Boy is.

I started building Colorado Boy in Ridgway in the summer of 2008. My goal was to have a small corner pub where locals could meet over a pint. Given that the population of Ridgway was only 800, I planned on a 7 BBL system, which I determined would be more than enough to supply the beer needs in our tiny mountain community.

When we opened in December that year, the economy was going over the cliff like Thelma & Louise, but with a smile on our face we opened the doors anyway and hoped for the best.

It took about six months to realize that there just weren't enough people to survive on cold beer and popcorn alone, so after experimenting with Panini sandwiches, we switched our format to Neapolitan-style pizza to bring more people through the door. More people, more beer. I had been doing pizza since my early brewing days in 1993.

We also started teaching a formal immersion class on how to build breweries. More than simply a hands-on class for would-be brewery owners, the immersion class was an initiation to a mentorship program. This approach has been very successful in helping to open over 70 breweries in the US and abroad.

During this time we also began working with a local welder to build affordable brew houses based on our model for brewing. Tom Bennett of Bennett Forgeworks has now grown into a major player in the U.S. manufacturing of brewing equipment.

Colorado Boy has since expanded down the road to Montrose, Colorado. There, we have incorporated much of what we teach in the immersion class, which is now also taught at Big Choice Brewing in Broomfield, Colorado and Echo Brewing in Frederick, Colorado.

The following is an overview of Colorado Boy in Ridgway and Montrose to help you understand how our SOPs have developed. I have included suppliers of equipment, because I would want to know that information if I were reading this. The figures are correct at the time of writing.

Colorado Boy Ridgway

Our Ridgway location is in the small historic section of Ridgway, Colorado. Originally a drug store, our location was built in 1915.

When we took over the space, it was one large room with a small restroom in the back corner. It had 1,000 sq. ft. on the main floor and 200 sq. ft. in the basement.

We located the brewery in the front of the building because the floor joists were sitting right on the ground, which allowed us to remove the floor, add plumbing, and pour a new floor that could support the brewing equipment weight.

The remainder of the space went for the bar, small seating area, tiny kitchen, and one restroom. The basement has been used for our office and storage.

With limited space for a brewing facility, we located the cooler that housed the serving tanks directly behind the bar so that the tap lines would not need to be refrigerated with a separate glycol system, but rather could go through the wall right to the taps.

Originally, there was no hot liquor tank or mill. We created hot water for sparge in the kettle and stored it in the fermenter that we would use each day. We used a separate home brew March pump to move the water out of the fermenter as our sparge. For grain, we bought our grain pre-milled, which increased our cost by $0.05 per pound.

Currently, we use a storage tank for our lot liquor that we have on a platform so that we can gravity the water to the sparge. The water is still heated by the brew kettle so there is no separate heating system for the tank.

We worked with Tom Bennett of Bennett Forgeworks to design an affordable mill that could work in a limited space. It now sits under the hot liquor tank and has a flex auger attached to transport the grist above the mash tun where it falls through a grist hydrator and into the mash. This system makes brew day an easy one-person job.

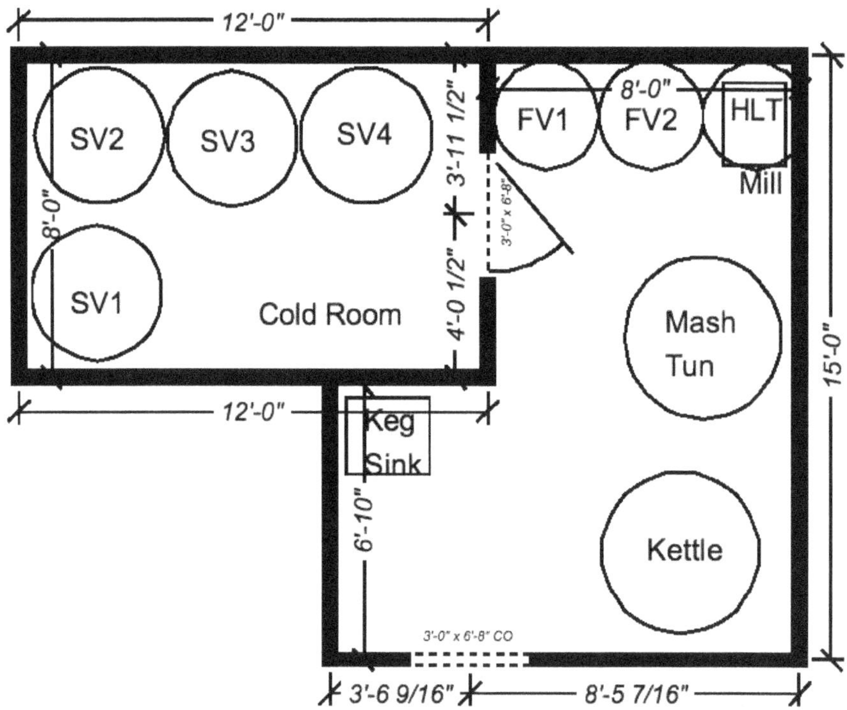

Ridgway Brew House

Ridgway Cold Storage

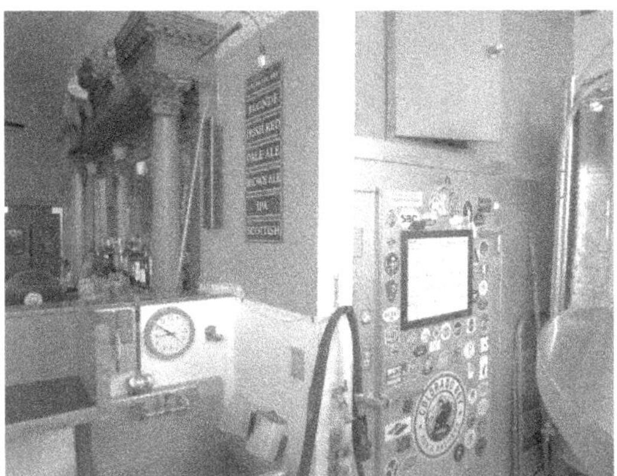

Ridgway Cold Storage Directly behind Bar

Colorado Boy Brewing Equipment List

7 BBL Brew Kettle – Used Cross Distributing Kettle
7 BBL Mash Tun – Bennett Forgeworks uninsulated
500 liter Hot Liquor Tank on stand – Letina
2 x 1000 liter Letina fermentation tanks
4 x 7 BBL Chinese Serving Tanks
Mill - Bennett Forgeworks
Flex Auger – Farmer Boy AG
Grist Hydrator – Specific Mechanical
Used Kayak paddle - Free
Thomsen sanitary pump with ¾ HP motor - Probrewer
Heat Exchanger 1 – Used Alfla Lavel
Heat Exchanger 2 – Used Lafranchi Milk Chiller
Grant – Used keg with TC added to bottom side
Hot hose – Five Star Chemicals (20 ft.)
Transfer Hose – GW Kent Clear Nutriflo (50 ft)
Glycol Set Up – Foxx Equipment UBC Chiller ¾ hp.
½ BBL and 5 gallon kegs – Used various places
Oxygenating Stone Set Up – GW Kent
Pressure Relief Valves (4) – GW Kent
Carbonating Stones (4)– GW Kent

Colorado Boy Montrose

Originally the idea in Montrose was strictly a pizzeria with beer that would be supplied by our Ridgway location. However, after only one summer, it was easy to see that Ridgway could not produce enough beer for two busy locations.

Colorado Boy in Montrose is 3,750 sq. ft., which we divided equally between back kitchen and front dining room. There was more than ample space to install a 7 BBL brewing operation. The significant difference from Ridgway was that the cold storage room could not be next to the bar, so we would need to utilize a glycol trunk line from where the serving tanks would be to the taps at the bar.

We decided to build the brew house, including fermentation, in the back kitchen and, separately, build a cold room in the dining area so that the serving tanks would not only be closer to the taps, but they would also be visible to the customers.

In the dining room, there is a wood floor on top of slab concrete. Fortunately, the plumbing for the floor drain in the bar ran directly under the location for the cold room. All we needed to do was tear up the wood floor, locate the drain pipe, and hook up a new floor drain. Next, we poured new concrete, being careful to adequately slope the floor to the drain.

The walls were built with 2x6 construction and were super insulated. For the door, we used a simple sliding glass patio door. Refrigeration was added on the top of the cold room.

Given the narrowness of the dining room (25 ft.), the cold room with the serving tanks is only 6 ft. wide and 16 ft. long. This would give us enough room for 5 tanks. The brew house is wider at 10 ft. and 16 ft. long.

Since there was already a flat concrete floor in the back kitchen, we cut out a small area to install a trench drain, then poured a new 4-in. concrete floor on top of the existing floor that also would flow to the drain.

Simple walls were added to sequester the brew house. A roof was left off since the ceiling height in the kitchen is 14 ft. Leaving the brew house open at top also helped with air flow and allowed us to use existing light that was already on the ceiling in the existing kitchen.

Colorado Boy Montrose Brewing Equipment

7 BBL Brew Kettle – Bennett Forgeworks
7 BBL Mash Tun – Bennett Forgeworks
500L Hot Liquor Tank – Letina
2 x 7 BBL Conical Fermenters – Chinese
5 x 5 BBL Serving Tanks – Chinese
Mill – Bennett Forgeworks
Thomsen Pump ¾ HP – Probrewer
Heat Exchanger 1 – CPE Systems
Heat Exchanger 2 – Hamby Dairy
Glycol Chiller – Foxx Equipment ¾ HP
Hot Hose (20 ft) – Five Star Chemical
Transfer Hose (100 ft) Nutriflo – GW Kent
Oxygen Stone Set Up – GW Kent
Grist Hydrator – Bennett Forgeworks
Grant – Bennett Forgeworks
Mash Paddle – Kayak paddle
Pressure Relief Valves (7) – Chinese
Carbonation Stone (5) GW Kent
Assorted 5 and 15 gallon kegs - Used

The entire cost to add the brewery to the restaurant, which includes equipment, build-out, and refrigeration was approximately $75,000.

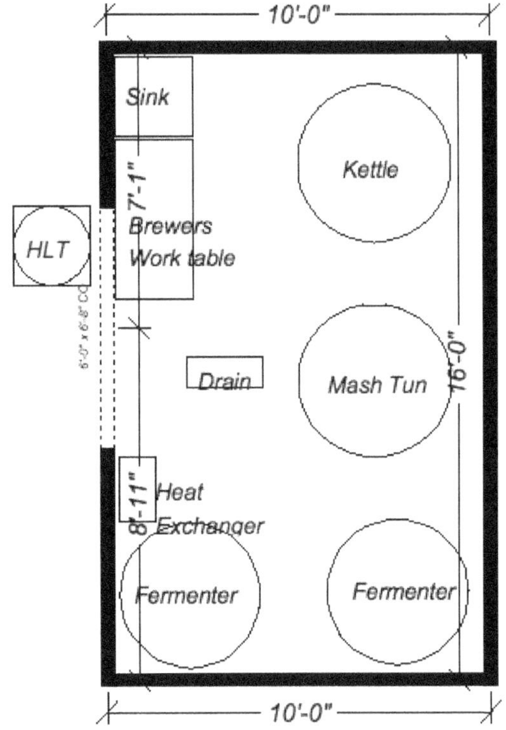

Colorado Boy Montrose Brew House

Montrose Brew House

Hot Liquor Tank Seen in Upper Left

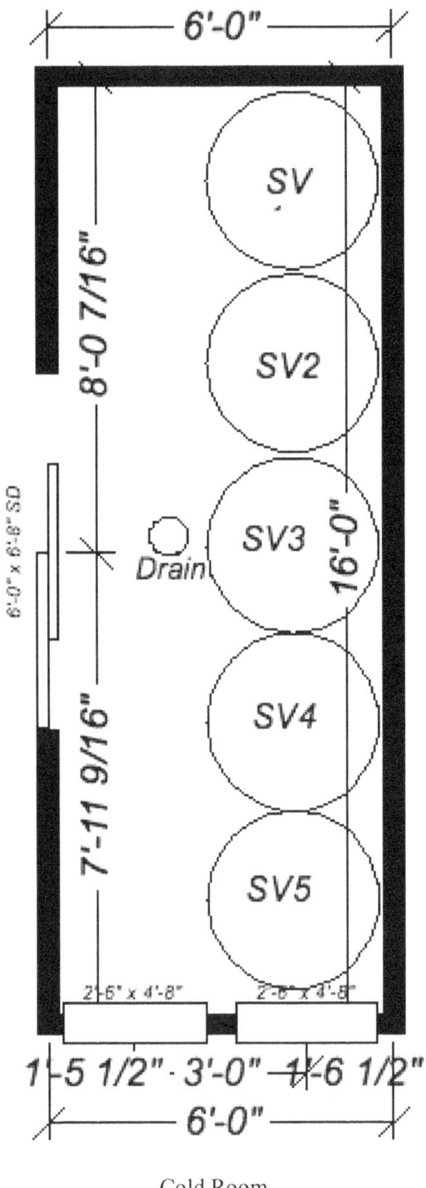
6'-0"
SV
SV2
SV3
SV4
SV5
Drain
8'-0 7/16"
7'-11 9/16"
16'-0"
6'-0" x 6'-8" SD
2'-6" x 4'-8"
2'-6" x 4'-8"
1'-5 1/2"
3'-0"
1'-6 1/2"
6'-0"

Cold Room

Montrose Cold Room

Sliding Glass Patio Doors

Appendix: Peer Reviewers

Before publishing our SOP, I wanted to have it reviewed by other professional brewers just to make sure that the methods I use are consistent with what others are using.

The feedback I received was very helpful in acknowledging that our methods were good and in making some changes that were recommended as well.

Without the help of the following brewers, I would not have the confidence in this little manual that I do. To them, I am very grateful.

Wayne Waananen
Station 26 Brewing - Denver, CO

Chuck Skypeck
Technical Brewing Projects Manager
Brewers Association

Jack Buttrum, Oil Horse Brewing
Longview, Texas

Bryan Selder, Post Brewing
Lafayette, CO

Scott Bruslind & Matt Cowart
Conversion Brewing – Lebanon, Oregon

Randy King
612 Brew
Minneapolis, MN

Seth Townsend
Liquid Mechanics Brewing
Lafayette, CO

In Addition:

Ro Guenzel
Great Divide Brewing – Denver, CO

Jason Weissburg
Assawoman Bay Brewing Co – Ocean City, Maryland

Leonard Schaeding
The Maple Grille – Hemlock, MI

About The Author

Tom Hennessy is the founder of seven breweries, including Il Vicino Brewing Co., Palisade Brewery, and Colorado Boy Brewery. Tom started brewing professionally in 1993. He is the author of the 1995 video *Frankenbrew*, and the 2013 book *Brewery Operations Manual*. Tom is also founder of the Colorado Boy Immersion Course, which has helped more than 70 students open breweries around the world.

More information about the Colorado Boy Immersion Course can be found at www.coloradoboy.com.

www.ingramcontent.com/pod-product-compliance
Lightning Source LLC
Chambersburg PA
CBHW031944190326
41519CB00007B/658

* 9 7 8 1 9 4 4 7 8 4 1 4 0 *